760

PROJECT

Paul Coo
performin
own poer
in cartoon
five-a-s

Jane Eccle:
London wi

Tongue Twisters
and
Tonsil Twizzlers

chosen by
Paul Cookson

and illustrated by
Jane Eccles

Patchwork Rap by Adrian Mitchell first published by Oberon Books.
Reprinted by permission of Peters Fraser and Dunlop.

MACMILLAN CHILDREN'S BOOKS

First published 1997 by
Macmillan Children's Books
a division of Macmillan Publishers Ltd
25 Eccleston Place London SW1W 9NF
Basingstoke and Oxford
www.macmillan.co.uk

ISBN 0 330 34941 4

12 14 16 18 17 15 13 11

A CIP catalogue record for this book is available from the British Library.

Typeset by Macmillan Children's Books
Printed by Mackays of Chatham PLC, Kent

Contents

Salestalk

She sells seashells on the seashore.
I've heard it before.

Well, he sells red leather weatherproofs
on the shop floor.
Nah! That's a bore.

Well, I hear tell
that she sells selfish shellfish
from the top shelf of the shelter
by the chip-shop door.
Hmm. Tell me more.

Well, let me just yell
that we sell swell yellow lollies
from red lorries
and big red brollies
from mellow yellow lorries,
the brollies
all wrapped rapidly
in big bright boxes of straw,
and the lollies
all linked loosely
in bunches of four.
Cor!..........................(What for?)

Tony Mitton

The Magician's Composition of a Spell of Great Precision

The magician with ambition was a mystical physician
who sought the composition of a spell of great precision.
For all things scientific
his knowledge was prolific:
voltage and transmission, gaseous ignition,
simple recognition of nuclear collision
and specific hieroglyphics was wicked and terrific.

This wizard of decision was a great mathematician,
a master statistician of addition and division.
For all things mathematical
his brain was acrobatical:
fractions and subtractions, factors and reactions,
equation complications, long multiplications,
computations problematical his mind was telepathical.

The solution's constitution was brought unto fruition,
magic spells and sorcery defying definition.
An amazing combination of enchanting calculations.
A wonderful creation beyond imagination.
A crazy composition of wish and superstition
fulfilling the ambition of this magician's vision
the lotions and the potions made him such a rich 'un
thanks to their transmission on national television.

Paul Cookson

Barry and Beryl the Bubble Gum Blowers

Barry and Beryl the bubble gum blowers
blew bubble gum bubbles as big as balloons.
All shapes and sizes, zebras and zeppelins,
swordfish and sealions, sharks and baboons,
babies and buckets, bottles and biplanes,
buffaloes, bees, trombones and bassoons
Barry and Beryl the bubble gum blowers
blew bubble gum bubbles as big as balloons.

Barry and Beryl the bubble gum blowers
blew bubble gum bubbles all over the place.
Big ones in bed, on backseats of buses,
blowing their bubbles in baths with bad taste,
they blew and they bubbled from breakfast till bedtime
the biggest gum bubble that history traced.
One last big breath . . . and the bubble exploded
bursting and blasting their heads into space.
Yes Barry and Beryl the bubble gum blowers
blew bubbles that blasted their heads into space.

Paul Cookson

Camilla Caterpillar

Camilla Caterpillar kept a caterpillar killer-cat.
A caterpillar killer categorically she kept.
But alas the caterpillar killer-cat attacked Camilla
As Camilla Caterpillar catastrophically slept.

Mike Jubb

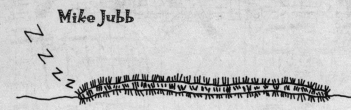

Tongue Twizzlers and Tonsil Twisters Leave Tongues Sizzled and Tonsils Blistered

Untwizzle your tongue unzip your lips
Untwist your tonsils get to grips
With rhyming rhythms for twisted tongues
Gonna rhyme those rhythms all day long
Gonna roll those rhythms rhyme those rocks
Gonna twist and tie your tongue in knots
Unroll your tongue turn up the watts
Unlock the locks on your voice box
Gonna shake your tonsils rattle your teeth
Roll vocal chords beyond belief
Twisted rhythms for rhyming tongues
Gonna rhyme those rhythms right not wrong
Tongue twizzlers and tonsil twisters
Leave tongues sizzled and tonsils blistered.

Paul Cookson and David Harmer

Patchwork Rap

I'm a touch lazy
Don't like doing much work
But often get the itch
To pitch into some patchwork
It may be a hotchpotch
Like fretwork or such work
When I slouch on my couch
And I fetch out my patchwork

First I snatch a patch
From the batch in my pouch
But the patch doesn't match
The patches on my patchwork
So I catch another patch
From the batch in my satchel
And this one matches
The patches on my patchwork.
So I take my patch
And attach it with stitches
Patch against patch
Where the patchwork matches
But if it doesn't match
Even after it's attached
Then the mismatched stitch
Has to be detached.

I don't like thatchwork
Don't like ditchwork
Only kind I favour
Is my patchwork stitchwork
And soon my patchwork's
Going like clockwork
Sharper than a pitchfork
Neater than brickwork
Hotter than a firework
Cooler than a waxwork.

So I snatch a patch
From the batch in my pouch
But the patch doesn't match
The patches on my patchwork
So I catch another patch
From the batch in my satchel
And this one matches
The patches on my patchwork.

So I take my patch
And attach it with stitches
Patch against patch
Where the patchwork matches
And I keep on patching
Till everything's matching
And I keep on stitching
Till I've filled up the kitchen
with my rich rich rich rich
Wider than a soccer pitch
Wonderful colourful patchwork quilt!

Now which stitch is which?

Adrian Mitchell

Shop Chat

My shop stocks:

> locks, chips,
> chopsticks,
> watch straps,
> traps, tops,
> taps, tricks,
> ship's clocks,
> lipstick and chimney pots.

What does your shop stock?

> *Sharkskin socks.*

Libby Houston

Peter Plunkett's Trumpet

Peter Plunkett plays a trumpet,
Peter plays all day.
Pete plays perfect piccolo
There's nothing Pete can't play.

Pete plays pan-pipes to perfection,
Pete plays rock and pop –
But Pete's poor pals just pray for peace
And plead with Pete to stop.

Pete's pal Paul said, 'Pack it in.'
But Pete replied, 'No fear.'
So Paul picked Peter's trumpet up
And pushed it in Pete's ear.

'Please Paul pull my trumpet out,'
Pete asked Paul politely.
But Paul just pushed it further in
And said, 'Not flippin' likely!'

Now Peter Plunkett plays his trumpet
In a style unique –
Pete puffs his trumpet through his ear
Instead of through his cheek!

Clive Webster

Lightning

I find lightning quite exciting,
Flickering, flashing, fearfully frightening,
Very vivid and inviting –
Bright white nightly lightning.

Twirling through the winter twilight,
Blazing, brilliant, blue-white, brightening,
Thunder threatening through the skylight –
Nightly sprightly lightning!

John Irwin

The Lithper'th Thtory

Thally Thornton'th thkinny thithter
Had the motht thtupendouth blithter.
Thuthan thought that they thould lanthe it.
Thally thaid, 'I thouldn't chanthe it!'
But Thuthan thouted, with thome thpirit,
'Thut up, Thally! Whothe heel ith it?'
Thally thaid, 'It'th yourth, thank heuventh.
I bet your thoeth are thithe eleventh!'

'Thtop thith noithe!' their mother thaid,
'And thtick thith plathter on inthtead.'

That made the pair of them dethitht!

(I hope *you* haven't got a lithp?)

Pam Gidney

Problems in the School of Fish

(An Inquisition with Fish In)

On the whole, would you say that a solo sole
should enrol in a shoal of sole?
Do the venomous antennae of anemones
menace many of their eminent enemies?

Well, I turned aside and sighed and denied it,
as a slightly short-sighted light-shy sea-slug
shrugged, wide-eyed, undecided.

Shall our six sick sharks, shivery and sallow,
seek shelter in the shadows of sandy shallows?
Is its purpleness surplus to the purpose of a porpoise?
Is the shorter sort of shore-turtle sure to be a tortoise?

Well, I turned aside and sighed and denied it,
while the slightly short-sighted light-shy sea-slug
shrugged, wide-eyed, undecided.

Should sea-shore shrimps shun sunshine?
And if it's customary to trust crustaceans,
surely surly shellfish shouldn't be so selfish?

As I turned aside and I sighed and denied it,
the slightly short-sighted light-shy sea-slug
still shrugged, wide-eyed, undecided.

Nick Toczek

Vlad

Vlad ve vampire
vlies vrough voonlight,
velvet vat vings
vlitter-vlutter.
Vlad's very vain
vith vangs vo vlong
vey vite vrough vlesh
vlike vutter.
Vlad vears a vast
vile violet vest

villed vith vermin
vrom ve vault
vich vongs vorse van
virty vultures —
vo vonder victims
vaint vand vall.
Vicious, vulgar,
vlood-vrinking, vad,
violent, villainous
vot a vlad!

Dave Calder

Gymnastic Jim's Gymnastical Gym

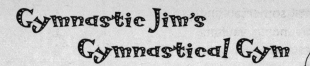

Gymnastic Jim's Gymnastical Gym
generates gymnasts lithe of limb
who skipping stay spectacularly slim,
throwing, thrusting, thinking thin,
keep on toning, keep in trim,
keep on training when they're in
Gymnastic Jim's Gymnastical Gym.

Gymnastic Jim's Gymnastical Gym
beefs up bodies pert and prim
with verve, vitality, vigour and vim,
supple sinews stretching skin,
slip and slide and splash and swim
it's goodbye gut when you're in
Gymnastic Jim's Gymnastical Gym.

Gymnasts jump and jog
Gymnasts jiggle and jig
Gymnasts juggle and joggle
Bodies bronzed and big.

Gymnasts put the shot
Gymnasts pull and push
Gymnasts punish muscles
With adrenaline rush.

Balancing beams, somersaulting,
swinging rings, running, vaulting,
stretching splits and never faulting
for a gymnast's most exalting.

Firm and fit not flabby and fat
Rough and tough and proud of that
Rippling torsos formed and flat
Gymnastic Jim's is where it's at.

Gymnastic Jim's Gymnastical Gym
generates gymnasts lithe of limb
who skipping stay spectacularly slim
and beef up bodies pert and prim
with verve, vitality, vigour and vim
keep on toning, keep in trim
keep on training when they're in
Gymnastic Jim's Gymnastical Gym.

Paul Cookson

The Demolition Giant

Dark stone released
this brick-built beast
man-made, mostly,
partly ghostly,
ghastly, towering,
overpowering:
a body based
on building waste
with every trace of flesh replaced.

He's firstly, lastly
ever so vastly
made out of debris.
He's rubbly, pebbly,
doubly, trebly
bigger than you and me.

Got bricks and dirt
inside his shirt,
great big boulders
for his shoulders,
sides of houses
in his trousers,
a sturdy belt
of grey asphalt
and a coat of old carpet and underfelt.

He's rumbly, grumbly,
terribly crumbly,
humbly tumbledown too.
He's rubbly, pebbly,
doubly, trebly
bigger than me and you.

In place of bones
are paving stones,
and all his veins
are pipes and drains
in which the blood's
a flood of mud,
while x-ray charts
reveal his heart's
old central heating boiler parts.

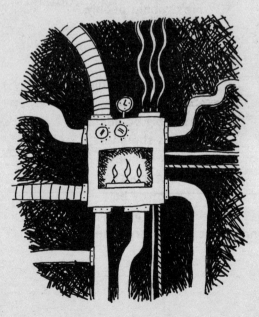

He differs from us.
He's broad as a bus,
taller than a tree.
He's rubbly, pebbly,
doubly, trebly
bigger than you and me.

They say his stride
is ten yards wide,
with concrete blocks
inside his socks.
His room-beam arms
have doorstep palms,
while bags of sand,
I understand,
form the fingers of each hand.

He's mumbly, bumbly,
somewhat stumbly,
one of the fumbly few.
He's rubbly, pebbly,
doubly, trebly
bigger than me and you.

His fireplace gob's
a cobbled job;
the teeth, in clumps
of crooked stumps,
are broken plates
and tiles and slates.
He grinds and grates,
and contemplates . . .
nothing at all . . . but stands and waits.

He's mouldy and old
and feels the cold.
We hardly reach his knee.
He's rubbly, pebbly,
doubly, trebly
bigger than you and me.

His hair's odd things
like ropes and strings
and old bed-springs,
long chains of rings
and wiry things.
It curls and clings,
then suddenly swings
and lifts, like wings,
and sparkles like the wealth of kings.

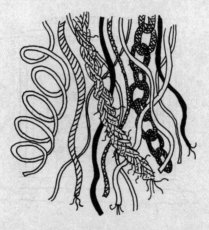

He's crusty, dusty,
dreadfully musty,
justifiably blue.
He's rubbly, pebbly,
doubly, trebly
bigger than me and you.

His face ain't quaint.
It's peeling paint,
with brash moustache
that's bits of trash.
His dim eyesight's
frosted skylights.
And when he blows
that chimney nose
a sort of sooty slime fills his hankie, I suppose.

Cos firstly, lastly
ever so vastly
he's made of debris.
He's rubbly, pebbly,
doubly, trebly
bigger than you and me.

Nick Toczek

Double Trouble Twins

For our sins,
My brother and I are called the:

Double quick,
Double slick;
Double dealing,
Double squealing;
Double thinking,
Double blinking;
Double jointed,
Double pointed;
Double meaning,
Double scheming;
Double talking,
Double squawking
DOUBLE TROUBLE TWINS!

(Which doesn't exactly cover us in glory,
But we say there are two sides to every story!)

Ian Souter

Little Lisa

Little Lisa likes to lick
lots and loads of lovely lollies
lime and lychees, melon, lemon,
lychees, lime and lemon, melon,
melon, lemon, lime and lychees,
lemon, melon, lychees, lime.

Licking lollies little Lisa
liked to lick Molly's lollies.
Licking lollies little Lisa
liked to lick Polly's lollies.
Licking lollies little Lisa
liked to lick Holly's lollies.
Molly's lollies, Polly's lollies,
Holly's lollies, jolly lollies
lots and loads and loads and lots
and lots and loads and loads and lots
and lots of lovely jolly lollies
Little Lisa liked to lick.

Little Lisa liked to lick
Lots of lovely jolly lollies
nicked the licks from Molly's lollies
licked the nicks from Polly's lollies
quickly licked Holly's lollies
slickly licked lots of lollies
lemon lollies
melon lollies
lychee lollies
lime lollies
lots and lots of lovely lollies
Little Lisa liked to lick.

David Harmer

Fishing for Fellas

Flora and Frannie from Forfar
And Florrie and Fanny from Fyfe
Went fishing for fellas in Falmouth
To hook 'em and have 'em for life.

Flora was first to strike lucky,
She found a fab fella called Frankie,
A factory foreman from Feltham,
Whose frame was all long, lean and lanky.

Frannie found Freddie from Fulford,
Friendly and forty and fair,
Florrie got fixed up with Ferdie
Who fell in a flash for her hair.

Finally Fanny found fortune
With a farmer from Farnsworth called Phil,
He said that her fantasy figure
Fired in him a fabulous thrill.

FANNY ♡ PHIL

It all fitted in to perfection –
Fanny and Phil went to Fyfe,
Frankie, the foreman from Feltham
Went back there with Flora his wife.

Frannie from Forfar got married
To Freddie from Fulford and then
Finally Florrie and Ferdie
Were wed down in Falmouth. Amen.

Clive Webster

FRANNIE ♡ FREDDIE

Wurd Up

Blowin like a hurricane
Destroyin all the competishan
Kickin up the lirix hard
There ain't no opposishan
Coz
Wen I'm on a roll like this
I'm jus like a physishan
Like a boxer . . . punch you out
With lirical precishan
Flowing like a river
Jus
Flyin like a bird
'N'
Checkin out the ridim
Jus takin in my wurdz
It's time
Ter climb
'n' rime
The sign
Jus grows
'n' flows
'n' shows
'n' throws
a skill
Ter thrill
'n' kill

Jus chill
Coz
I'm
Stingin like a nettle
Jus bitin like a flea
Smoother than a baby's skin
Much ruffer than the sea
Colder than an icicle
Hotter than the sun
Lirix always on the move
Like bullets from a gun
Much noisier than thunder
Much cooler than the rain
I'm fitter than an exercise
Deep within the brain
Sharper than a needle
More solid than a rock
Repeatin like an echo
As rhythmic as a clock
More dangerus than a lion
Much louder than a plane
As quite as a whisper
I burn yer like a flame
Faster than a jaguar
Slower than a snail
Yeah! rapid like a heartbeat
Tuffer than a nail
More painful than a scratch
As tasty as food
Horrible like a medicine

My lirix change yer mood
As tasty as a mango
As bitter as a lime
Softer than a coconut
Endless as the time
Kickin like a reggae song
Much sadder than the blues
I'm as tirin as a marathon
Give yer all the news
Wilder than a stampede
As gentle as a breeze
Irritatin as a cough
More wicked than a sneeze
More lively than a child
Romantic that's me
Still harsh like the winter
Jus buzzin like a bee
The rimes 'n' times are signs
to blow 'n' show a flow

The wurdz

WURD UP!

Martin Glynn

Pasting Patsy's Pasty Posters

Petra Porter pastes in precincts
Patsy's pasty pasties posters
Patsy's posters for her pasties
And her tasty pastry pasta.

Patsy pays a pretty penny
For Petra's posters in the precincts
But Paula pastes her posters faster
Passes Petra, pasting past her.

So Patsy's posting Paula's posters
paying pasty Paula plenty
for faster pasta poster pasting
pasting pasta posters faster.

David Harmer

37

Charlie on the Telly

Charlie Chaplin's on the telly.

Willy's watching Charlie
shilly shally with a trolley
what a silly billy Charlie!

Sally's watching Willy
with a plate of wobbly jelly
watching Charlie on the telly.
Charlie's fallen roly-poly
down a hilly in a valley.

Nelly's juggling with a plate of wiggly vermicelli
watching Sally watching Willy
watching silly billy Charlie
dilly dally on the telly
with a really pally Collie.
Willy's wriggly
Sally's giggly.

Nelly's calling Kylie
(smiley Kylie) who is shyly
watching Nelly
watching Sally
watching Willy
watching Charlie being silly on the telly.

Kylie's calling Molly
and Molly's calling Polly
(who is truly very jolly)
saying Nelly, Sal and Willy
are getting really giggly
watching Charlie on the telly
struggle with a woolly pully.

Billy . . . no I'd better stop
'cos this is getting silly.

Gerard Benson

P.S. A list of characters not included in this poem:
    Millie, Kellie, Ali, Wally, Julie, Holly, Ollie, Shelley,
    Tilly, Shirley, Mali, Dolly, Hayley, Gilly, Ellie, Lily,
    Solly and Jim.

Dick's Dog

Dick had a dog
The dog dug
The dog dug deep
How deep did Dick's dog dig?

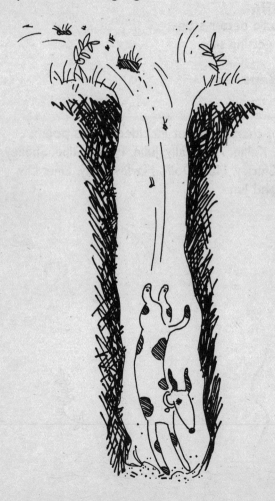

Dick had a duck
The duck dived
The duck dived deep
How deep did Dick's duck dive?

Dick's duck dived as deep as Dick's dog dug.

Trevor Millum

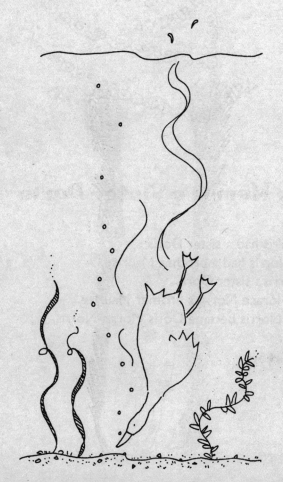

Boris Morris's Sister Doris

Boris Morris had a sister Doris.
Horace Norris had a brother Maurice.
Boris Morris's sister Doris
Married Horace Norris's brother Maurice.
So Doris Norris became Doris Morris-Norris.

John Foster

Iffy Sniffy

Sue smells sewer smells
Sitting by the street-side.
The sewer smells that Sue smells
Are never on the sweet side.

The sewer smells are sour smells.
They're make-you-wish-for-a-shower smells,
Those sewer smells that Sue smells
When she's sitting by the street-side.

John Kitching

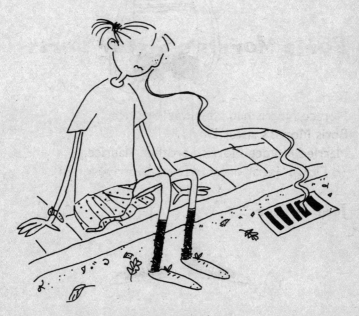

Shaun Short's Short Shorts

Shaun Short bought some shorts.
The shorts were shorter than Shaun Short thought.
Shaun Short's short shorts were so short,
Shaun Short thought, 'Shaun, you ought
Not to have bought shorts so short.'

John Foster

Breakfast for One

Hot thick crusty buttery toast
Buttery toasty thick hot crust
Crusty buttery hot thick toast
Crusty thick hot toasty butter
Thick hot buttery crusty toast
Toasty buttery hot thick crust
Hot buttery thick crusty toast –

With marmalade is how I like it most!

Judith Nicholls

Poem about food written by a man who had a problem with the computer key that comes between K and M so he had to use T instead

Tucy and Bitty tove tiquorice,
Tenny and Testie do not,
Taura and Timmy tike tangerines,
Do Tarry and Ten?
Not a tot.
Tinda and Terry tick totties,
Temon and Time
On a stick,

Tommy and Jutie think jetty
Is tikety to make you feet sick.
Taurence and Teddy tike custard that's tumpy,
With a tovety skin on the top,
Terry and Testor tike jettied eets
but Tionet says it's
Just stop.

David Orme

Kate's Cakes

Kate can cook quite good cakes.
Quite good cakes Kate can cook.
Cup cakes, currant cake, chocolate chips,
cheesecakes, cherry cakes shaped like ships.
Try Katie's truffle cakes, custard cups as well,
cream cakes, queen cakes capped with caramel,
curds, coffee, coconut, decorated cakes,
chunky cakes, chewy cakes, cocoa cakes with flakes.

That Kate can cook quite good cakes
quite clearly there's no question –
but can Kate cure a case
of chronic indigestion?

Jill Townsend

Pyramid

```
            P
           EAK
          PLACE
         PROUDLY
        PROVIDING
       PRESTIGIOUS
      PLUSH PRIVATE
     PILED PENTHOUSE
    PERFECTLY PLANNED
   PANORAMIC POSITION
  PART PAYMENT POSSIBLE
 PAST PHARAOHS PREFERRED
```

Dave Calder

The Secret Lives of Teachers

Revealing rhymes about what teachers do in their spare time
chosen by Brian Moses

What Teachers Wear In Bed!

It's anybody's guess
what teachers wear in bed at night
so we held a competition
to see if any of us were right.

We did a spot of research,
although some of them wouldn't say,
but it's probably something funny
as they look pretty strange by day.

Our Headteacher's quite old-fashioned,
he wears a Victorian nightshirt,
our sports teacher wears her tracksuit
and sometimes her netball skirt.

We asked our secretary what she wore
but she shooed us out of her room,
and our teacher said, her favourite nightie
and a splash of expensive perfume.

And Mademoiselle, who teaches French,
is really very rude,
she whispered, '*Alors*! Don't tell a soul,
but I sleep in the . . . back bedroom!'

Brian Moses

Parent-Free Zone

Poems about parents and other problems
chosen by Brian Moses

Victoria's Poem

Send me upstairs without any tea,
refuse me a plaster to stick on my knee.

Make me kiss Grandpa who smells of his pipe,
make me eat beetroot, make me eat tripe.

Throw all my best dolls into the river.
Make me eat bacon and onions – with liver.

Tell Mr Allan I've been a bad girl,
rename me Nellie, rename me Pearl.

> But don't, even if
> the world suddenly ends
>   ever again,
>   Mother,
> wipe my face with a tissue
> in front of my friends.

Fred Sedgwick

Nothing Tastes Quite Like a Gerbil

and other vile verses chosen by David Orme

Nothing Tastes Quite Like a Gerbil

Nothing tastes quite like a gerbil
They're small and tasty to eat –
Morsels of sweet rodent protein
From whiskers to cute little feet!

You can bake them, roast them or fry them,
They grill nicely and you can have them en croute,
In garlic butter they're simply delicious
You can even serve them with fruit.

So you can keep your beef and your chicken,
Your lamb and your ham on the bone,
I'll have gerbil as my daily diet
And what's more – I can breed them at home!

Tony Langham

Custard Pie
Poems that are jokes that are poems
Chosen by Pie Corbett

Love Poem

Her eyes were bright
as she reached out
and touched me with her
smooth, white hand.

I trembled,
excitedly;
as she happened
to be clutching
a live electric cable,
at the time.

Harry Munn

A selected list of poetry books available from Macmillan

The prices shown below are correct at the time of going to press. However, Macmillan Publishers reserve the right to show new retail prices on covers which may differ from those previously advertised.

All Macmillan titles can be ordered at your local bookshop or are available by post from:

Book Service by Post
PO Box 29, Douglas, Isle of Man IM99 1BQ

Credit cards accepted. For details:
Telephone: 01624 675137
Fax: 01624 670923
E-mail: bookshop@enterprise.net

Free postage and packing in the UK.
Overseas customers: add £1 per book (paperback)
and £3 per book (hardback).